Survival:
Disappear Without Trace, Find Food, Build Shelter, Filter Water And Start A Fire In The Deepest Wilderness

NATHAN CRAIG

Copyright © 2016 Nathan Craig

All rights reserved.

ISBN: 1537693840

ISBN-13: 978-1537693842

TABLE OF CONTENT

Introduction 7

Chapter 1 – Finding Food & Water 10

Plants 11

Insects 12

Eggs 13

Fishing 14

Meat 15

Water 16

Chapter 2 – Shelter 20

Chapter 3 – The Fire and other Essential Survival Tips 25

Flint and Steel 25

Rubbing 26

The Drill 27

Essential Tip 1 - North 28

Essential Tip 2 – Natural resources 29

Essential Tip 3 – Defenses 29

Essential Tip 4 - Signaling 30

Conclusion 31

Introduction

It may not be an image which crosses your mind often but it is possible for anyone to end up lost in the wilderness. It may seem a remote prospect but if you travel by car, plane or boat it is a fact of life that you are at risk of having an accident. This can result in you being injured and thrown from your vehicle or even the lone survivor of a plane which has crashed in bad weather off the beaten track and it is unlikely to be found for several days. In fact, the more you consider how you can become lost in the wilderness the more you will see that it is not only possible but that it happens to many people every year. A little preparation and some common sense can make a huge difference to your survival rate.

Of course, you may assume that it is best to wait with your vehicle; this will ensure help will locate you. However, if help is not able to get to you for several days you may have to consider the merits of staying in one spot versus the risk of travelling and locating food and water. There are other reasons why you may choose to leave your vehicle; it may be damaged and unable to provide you with a safe haven, it may be in a dangerous spot which is liable to put your life at risk; especially if it is attractive to wildlife. You may even simply be disorientated and wander away from the vehicle and not be able to find your way back. Simply stating that it will never happen to you means you will not engage in some basic preparation; your life may end up being in danger because you refused to believe it was possible.

The fact of the matter is that many people become stranded every year and must survive on their own; being prepared can make your task a little easier and increase your chance of survival.

There are several critical factors which can make the difference between whether you survive or not. One of the most important things you will need is somewhere to sleep; preferably a shelter from dangerous animals. This should be combined with a fire to ensure you stay warm and animals are kept at bay. You will also need food, the body can actually survive without food for an extended period of time, but, eating will provide a moral and spiritual boost. Alongside this, water is an essential item for your body. The human body can only last for a short space of time without water; it is essential to locate water and clean it if necessary to ensure it is toxin free.

Finally, knowing how to source these items, even in the deepest wilderness will increase your chances of survival and allow you to focus on becoming rescued. It is important to note that although there are times when it is better to stay with any vehicle, it will often not be enough if you are lost for more than just a few days. Follow the tips in this book to ensure you will be able to survive no matter what situation you find yourself in.

Chapter 1 – Finding Food & Water

Thankfully nature is good at providing sources of food and water. Even in the wilderness or where there appears to be no sign of life you may be surprised at the range of options available to you. Food does not actually need to be your first priority. As already mentioned it is possible to survive for weeks without any food. However, trying to do so will quickly affect your mental and physical ability to do even the simplest of tasks. It is also essential to provide you with a source of energy which will enable you to do the more essential tasks such as collecting firewood or maintaining your water reserves. It also helps to maintain a normal body temperature.

However, the most important role of food is to maintain your mental wellbeing. This is important as you need to have a clear head in order to make the right decision; one of the biggest ones is whether to stay in one spot or to continue to move; making it harder for rescuers to find you.

There are a variety of potential sources of food:

Plants

There are very few places which do not have flora and fauna growing all around you. Of course, not all of it is edible but there are a surprising number of everyday plants which can help to nourish your body.

The first rule to learn is that any plant which has a milky sap or white berries is generally not going to be a good choice; it will either poison you or make you very ill. Ideally you should familiarize yourself with a couple of plants which are edible before you get stuck in the wilderness. However this may not be possible, in which case, if you are not sure about whether a plant or berry is edible it is advisable to do a taste test. This is where you test a plant by eating a small piece of the plant or berry and then waiting at least half a day to make sure you do not get sick. Even then it is important to eat the berry or plant slowly; just to be certain.

Depending upon where you are and what time of year it is there are a range of fruits, berries and nuts which may be present and can be consumed. By starting your food search early you will have time to check and even prepare them. Plants which can be eaten include dandelion, burdock, asparagus, chickweed, fireweed and even sheep sorrel.

Insects

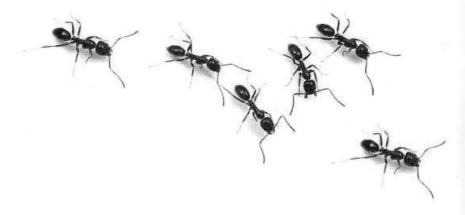

It is very difficult to find yourself anywhere where there is not some form of insect life. They can usually be found under rotten logs or in the bark of a tree. They are also especially common in dark and moist areas. The good news is that almost all insects are edible;

although you may not wish to eat them, but this is more of a cultural thing. Some of the easiest to find and catch are ants, worms, crickets and even grasshoppers. It is possible to eat them raw although you may find them harder to stomach. It is safer and easier for you mentally to cook them. This can be done by boiling them or even roasting them. Insects are an excellent form of protein and many of them have an acceptable flavor; they will go perfectly with your salad of dandelion leaves.

Eggs

Consuming bird eggs is one of the safest food sources you can find whilst in the wilderness; if you have created fire and have water you may even be able to boil them! Although your first instinct may be to look up, there are many birds which build their nests on the ground. Some will even put their eggs in a hole on the floor. Whether the nest is in the tree or on the floor, you need to use caution when taking the eggs; the bird they belong to may not be keen on giving them up.

It is worth noting that most countries do not allow you to collect and eat wild bird eggs; this must only be done in a real survival situation.

Fishing

Fish are an excellent source of protein, carbohydrates and even a variety of vitamins. Of course, you need to be near a stream in order to benefit from this option; something that will certainly help with your survival as this is a good source of water! Of course, if you are surviving in the wilderness you may not have any fishing gear with you. This means you will need to find an alternative way of catching your dinner.

One of the most common approaches in the wild is to use a small stick and whittle each end to a point; this can then be placed on the end of a makeshift line. If you do not have any strong string or twine you will need to locate a sturdy vine or similar to tie you make shift hook onto. You can then find bait from near the river; worms are usually a good starting point. Finally, you will need patience. In the hotter weather fish will generally be in deeper, cooler waters whilst in the colder weather they are likely to be nearer the surface enjoying the heat of the sun. Drop your bait in next to them and wait. Of course, your 'string' will need to be attached to a rod, a good stick, or reasonable sized tree branch will suffice for this.

Fish can make an excellent meal when cooked; you may even forget you are surviving in the wilderness for a moment!

It is worth noting that the survival bracelet, which comes in a variety of designs, is intended for situations like this. It is made from paracord and can be unraveled to create a long piece of strong rope; idea for a wide variety of uses when surviving in the wild.

If there is nothing else available you can simply use a branch, preferably 'Y' shaped to support pants or some other item of clothing; this can make an excellent fishing net.

Meat

The obvious solution to the need for food is to hunt the wildlife around you. However, this is not always the best solution. Unless you are already aware of the types of animals you will find and the best way to hunt them then you will use a lot of your time and energy attempting to kill an animal; quite possibly without any success. There is also an increased risk of injury which you should try hard to avoid when trying to survive. Instead, you are best to put several traps down; these can be simply holes dug deep enough so an animal cannot escape, or a cage made from branches which will drop from a tree when the animal passes under and knocks the branch whilst consuming the bait. Again, this is a skill which requires time and patience, but, a trap can be set and left, allowing you to complete other survival needs.

Perhaps the best way to prepare for either being stranded in the wilderness or intentionally disappearing is to familiarize yourself with what is edible and what is not; you can even undertake short trips with emergency back-up supplies in case you have any issues.

Water

Whilst food is essential to keep your energy and morale high, water is essential to simply stay alive. This is one of the most important things you will need to locate as soon as you realize you are lost in the wilderness. There are many different ways of finding water, depending upon your situation. If you are near a stream you have the best option available. Fast flowing water is much less likely to have harmful bugs in, a pond or lake will be relatively stagnant and will, therefore, potentially be full of bacteria.

There are two key elements regarding water:

1. Finding Water

If you are lucky enough to have found a pool of water then you will be able to move onto stage two. However, if there is not any water obviously available you will be faced with a choice of whether to establish a base and find water another way, or to keep walking until you locate some. This decision will be influenced by whether you are aiming to walk back to civilization or if you think you will be found by a rescue team.

Flowing water will normally find a channel at the bottom of a valley, you will need to head downhill to locate this; if you do not have time for this, or you are unable or willing to travel that distance you can dig a hole in the ground. You will need to find something that will collect water in it, a bowl, or your hat with a piece of plastic wrapped inside it. This is placed inside the hole and a clean cloth draped across the hole. This will need to be left overnight where condensation will collect in the cloth and drip into the bowl. You will also be able to wring out the cloth to gain valuable extra water. Another alternative to this is simply looking for plants which have big leaves capable of capturing water; they are likely to be covered in dew drops first thing in the morning.

2. Treating or Filtering Water

Once you have located the water you will need to ensure it is clean and safe to drink. If you are desperate a running stream is likely to be safe to drink, it is better to be sure. There are two approaches to ensuring the water is safe to drink, unless you happen to have any water purification tablets with you. The first is simply to boil it; you will need to create a fire and have something to boil the water in. Boiling for several minutes will kill all bacteria.

If fire is not an option you will be able to filter your water. The first thing you will need to do is create a cone from bark; birch is best but most trees will suffice. The bark can be lashed together with vines or a little paracord, if you have some. There should be a small hole at the bottom. The cone is then progressively filled with grass, then sand and then charcoal. You can repeat this layering as much as you like until you have filled the cone up. Water is poured in the top and a few moments later it will start to trickle out of the bottom, clean and ready to drink!

Chapter 2 – Shelter

The wilderness can be tough to survive in, hot days will often give way to cold nights and there are a variety of animals which may or not present a threat to you. You will also be open to the elements, rain will do more than just get you wet, it can seriously lower your body temperature and make you ill as well as lowering your morale. The solution is to create yourself a shelter, not only will it keep the worst of the elements off you, it will provide you with a feeling of security which will help you to sleep.

The first thing you will need to do is scour the landscape for any natural shelters, caves can be excellent as they are dry and easy to heat with a fire. However, you will have to be certain that the cave is unoccupied before you set yourself up in there. If there is no suitable natural shelter then you should locate a spot with trees relatively close to the water. You will then be able to strap one long branch to two trees. You can use your paracord or vine. This is the roof line; you will then need to put sticks going diagonally from this wood to the ground. Start with four or five and then add a couple of cross sticks, threading them through the first five if possible. You can then add lots more diagonal sticks to completely cover the end. To ensure it is secure it should all be tied together. The diagonal sticks should continue round each end of the shelter, leaving only one side open to the elements. Once this has been created you will need to cover your masterpiece; pine leaves offer extra protection but any kind of leaf or moss can be used; it will help to ensure the rain rolls off the shelter and keep the inside warm. You can also use moss or pine leaves to create a bed inside. This is important as if you are in direct contact with the ground your body will quickly lose heat

You will now have created a safe area where you can sleep and stay warm. This is also useful if you need somewhere to rest during the day. If you are planning on staying in one spot you can extend this by adding diagonal sticks to the front edge of the shelter; effectively turning it into a tent with just one small entrance. The idea place to put your fire is just outside your entrance, or open side. Close enough to enjoy the warmth but not close enough to set your shelter on fire!

This is not the only method of creating a shelter; if you are carrying anything with you, such as a big sheet or tarpaulin you could use that to make the shelter. Simply drape it over a log between two trees and use either rocks or rope to hold it down making an impromptu tent. However, tarpaulin is also an excellent vapor barrier and can be used to collect water as well as a variety of other tasks; even if you have some it may be more sensible to build a shelter from sticks and use the tarpaulin for other jobs.

Of course, this is just one option. If you are able to create a wigwam effect by leaning sticks together to create a circle and tying them together you will not need to use a tree as support. This can be handy if there are no trees suitable in the area but there are plenty of branches. Alternatively you can lean a long log at a forty five degree angle from the ground and support it with other logs to create a triangular shaped shelter. Both of these examples still need to be covered in leaves and moss to keep you warm and dry.

Of course, it is possible you will find yourself needing to survive in the snow without any trees nearby. You will then need shelter urgently to stay warm. The snow itself can be packed together around something you have which is moveable; such as a rucksack. Lie your backpack down and cover it with a piece or tarpaulin. Then pile snow on top of it. You will need to pack the snow tightly and make it roughly two feet deep all the way round as you create a half sphere. You can then open a small hole in one side of the dome and pull your gear out, excavating all the snow inside but keeping the walls at least two foot thick.

You will then have a very snug shelter to sleep in and regain your energy, as well as staying out of the elements. It is important to make sure the inside of your dome roof is smooth; this will stop, drips from falling on you. You will also need to have a raised area for your bed; it should be sloped at the sides to ensure any water drains away from your body.

Another alternative if you find yourself needing relief from intense sun is to use a tarpaulin to create a sun shade. In really hot climates you can layer the tarpaulin to create two roofs; they should be at least one foot apart. The air space between them will help to cool the hot air and provide better shade for you under both tarps.

The list of shelters which can be created with sticks, leaves and or a piece of tarpaulin is almost unlimited. The basic principle is that every roof needs to be covered with leaves and moss and even branches to keep the rain from hitting you whilst you rest. It will also help you to stay warm and, if it blends into its environment, it can be an effective way of keeping many animals away.

Creating your shelter is the first thing you need to do once you have decided where you will be staying the night; the amount of energy you expend in creating a structure should be as little as possible to create a good shelter and should also be in relation to whether it is for one night or longer term.

Chapter 3 – The Fire and other Essential Survival Tips

Whilst a shelter is essential, being able to create a fire will allow you to stay warm, cook food and even keep unwanted animals at bay. However, unless you happen to be carrying a box of matches or a lighter you will need to get your fire started the old fashioned way. In fact, there are a variety of different methods which can be employed to get your fire going:

Flint and Steel

It is highly likely that you will have something that is made of metal on your person; this can be a penknife or a belt buckle. Striking this with a piece of flint will create a spark. The spark can be used to ignite some very dry grass, or other type of kindling you have managed to locate. It is essential to have a quantity of kindling ready as well as a few slightly bigger sticks to help get the fire going properly. You will also need some sort of cloth to hold the flint with; this will prevent you from getting burned.

The sparks generated should land on your kindling and you will need to gently blow them to ensure the fire starts. As soon as you have a flame you can add a little more kindling.

Rubbing

If you do not have metal or are unable to find flint then you may be able to employ this method which uses just naturally found products. The first thing you will need to locate is a piece of hard wood; it will need to be roughly two inches thick. You will then need to gouge a straight line down the middle with it, your survival knife will do this easily but stone or similar object can work. The aim is to create a thin groove in the wood approximately quarter of an inch wide. You will then need to find a stick and create a point at one end of the stick. To create the heat necessary to start a fire you will need to run the stick the length of the groove in your wood with as much force as you can muster. The stick should remove tiny shavings from your wood base and these will be ignited by the heat of your movement. Again you will need to blow gently as you add tinder to your wood and coax the flame into existence.

The Drill

This uses a similar technique to rubbing but requires more practice to get it right. You will, again, need a stick which has a point on it, or you have created a point. You will then need to cut a small hole in the base board; this should be approximately an inch from the side. This is the point of a v shaped notch you will need to cut next. The V is then filled with your tinder to start your fire. The point of your stick is located in the hole at the peak of the V. You will then need to spin the stick by having one hand either side, constantly moving in opposite directions to each other whilst pushing the stick down.

After a few moments you should start to see smoke and you will be able to blow gently to encourage the flame into existence and add more tinder and wood.

There are a variety of other ways to start your fire, but these are the simplest for anyone new to starting fires. Of course, if you have glasses or a magnifying glass you will be able to amplify the sun's ray and create a fire. As with the other techniques, you are after smoke and then blowing gently with tinder to create a fire. It can be a good idea to practice these techniques in your own garden; this will ensure you have these skills if you ever need them.

Essential Tip 1 - North

Navigating may be one of the biggest issues you face if trying to find your way back to civilization. It can be easy to become disorientated and simply walk in a large circle. If you have found a river then you will be able to follow this; you will have a source of water, potential food and are likely to be heading towards civilization providing you follow the flow of the river.

However, you can also navigate by knowing where North is. At night time it is easy to work out which direction North is; simply look at the sky and locate the big dipper; there are two sides in line at one side; directly above these two is the North star and north.

Of course, if it is cloudy or daytime you will need to locate North via a different method. At the middle of the day the Sun is in the south, keeping the sun behind you will ensure you are heading north. You can also look at the trees to see which side has the most moss; this is an indication of north. Alternatively place a stick in the ground and mark where its shadow is. Then wait a little while and put the stick in the ground again and mark its shadow. You can then draw a line between the two marks which goes from east to west. You should then be able to look at the sun and assess which way it is moving; the opposite side of this is north.

Essential Tip 2 – Natural resources

There are an abundance of survival aids all around you, if you are prepared to look. For example, should you have been fortunate enough to have found a river then you will be able to follow it to find civilization. However, it may not be possible to keep it in sight at all times; depending upon the thickness of the woods. This is an opportunity to use the natural resources to lash several sturdy trees together to make a temporary raft. It is possible that the river will become too rough for a simple construction but it will move you much quicker and with a lot less energy than trekking through the undergrowth. Just be sure to take a sturdy stick with you to help you steer or row if necessary.

Essential Tip 3 – Defenses

One of the things that many people forget is that there are dangerous animals which exist in the wild. Even with a fire they may be tempted to come close and assess the possibilities. To avoid any incidents you should consider placing defenses around your perimeter; these should be far enough away to give you warning and close enough to see what you are dealing with.

A good defense can be achieved by circling your camp with bits of brush and small pieces of wood; no animal will be able to creep through without making a noise. You can also string up some wood or metal which will jangle against itself or another piece to make a distinctive noise. The aim is to ensure you are awake and can deal with any issue.

Essential Tip 4 - Signaling

If you are waiting to be rescued or walking but hoping to be discovered then you will need to be able to signal any rescuers. There are a variety of ways of doing this but it is important to have decided what you will do before they arrive. The smoke from a fire will always stand out on the landscape. If you have a mirror you can use it to bounce the sunlight back into the eyes of any pilot to ensure they know you are there; just don't do this for too long as you will blind them.

You may even be able to lay large logs into an SOS pattern in a clearing; you will need to assess the situation and decide the best course of action.

Conclusion

It may seem a daunting and particularly scary thought to find yourself alone in the wilderness and attempting to both survive and navigate your way back to society. However, it does not need to be! With a little planning you can keep your wits about you and create a means to stay alive whilst you either travel or wait to be rescued.

One of the most important factors to remember is that the worst thing you can do is panic. Your survival depends upon taking a few moments to assess your situation and calming deciding the best option to keep you alive. Despite the fact that water and food are essential the first priority should always be shelter; this will protect you from the elements. Extreme weather can kill long before you starve or even dehydrate. A shelter will allow you to remain warm and sleep properly which will help ensure you make rational decisions.

Although it may be against your nature, it is essential to check what equipment may be useful in any vehicle you were in and that anyone else was carrying; even if they have deceased the equipment may be of use to you. In order to increase your chances of survival should this scenario ever happen to you it is advisable to undertake some basic preparations now. The first of these is reading this book and learning the techniques described. You should always practice what you have learned to ensure you can do it in the wilderness.

You may also wish to consider buying and carrying a few basic survival tools:

- ✓ There are hundreds of different pocket knives available; you need want which is small and easy to hold. You should always keep it sharp.

- ✓ Paracord bracelets have become incredibly popular. They can be customized to suit your own image and they can be taken apart in a survival situation to provide a large amount of extremely strong and useful string.

- ✓ A small torch can be added to your key ring and may provide a valuable benefit if you find yourself lost in the wilderness at night. It will help you to navigate and see any threats before you create your shelter and fire.

You may feel that needing to survive in the wilderness is simply something which could not happen to you. However, it can and does happen to anyone, it is better to be prepared than to wish you had been!

Made in the USA
Middletown, DE
28 July 2021